STARTING

A

BUSINESS

QUICKSTART

GUIDE

Williams Brown

INTRODUCTION

You want to make sure you're prepared before starting work, but be aware that things will go wrong. To run a successful business, you need to adapt to changing circumstances.

Conducting in-depth market research on your niche and the demographics of your potential customers is an important part of creating a business plan. This includes conducting surveys, holding focus groups, and searching for SEO and social data.

Before you start selling your product or service, you need to build your brand and find people who are ready to jump in when you open the door for business.

This article is for entrepreneurs who want to learn the basics of starting a new business.

Things like naming your business and creating a logo are obvious, but what about other equally important steps? Whether you're setting up your business or creating a comprehensive marketing strategy, the workload can quickly add up. Instead of spinning your wheels and guessing where to start, follow this 10-step checklist to transform your business from a dream in your head to a real person

Intentionally left blank

CHAPTER ONE

HOW TO START A SMALL BUSINESS

This are quick start strategies
- Clear your mind
- Write a business plan
- Assess your finances
- Determine your legal structure
- Register with the government and the IRS
- Buy an insurance policy
- Create your team
- Choose your dealer
- Brand and promote yourself
- Grow your business

1. FLIRTER YOUR THINKING (CLEAR YOUR MIND)

If you want to start a business, you already have an idea of what you want to sell online, or at least the market you want to enter. Quickly search for companies in your chosen industry. Learn what brand leaders are doing today and determine how you can do it better. If you think your business can deliver something that other companies can't (or deliver the same thing, faster and cheaper), or you have a solid idea and are ready to draft a business plan.

Determine the "why".

"In the words of Simon Sinek, 'always start with why,' "Glenn Gutek, CEO of Hudang Konsultan and Asah, told Business News Daily. It may be wise to distinguish between the function of a personal reason or the market. Why, If you focus on meeting the needs of the market, the scope of your business will be greater than a business designed to serve personal needs."

See Franchise.

Another option is to open a franchise of an established company. The concept is that the brand already exists and the business model exists; All you need is a good location and funds to finance your operation.

Check the title of your project.

Regardless of the option you choose, it is important to understand why you are thinking. Stephanie Desaulniers, owner of Dezign's Business and former director of business and women's work programs at the Covation Center, advises entrepreneurs to avoid writing a business plan or business title before losing the value of their idea.

Intentionally left blank

CHAPTER TWO

EXPLAIN TO YOUR TARGET CUSTOMERS

Explain to your target customers.

Instead of taking time to think about who the customers will be and whether they want to buy or rent from them, Desaulniers says, people start their business.

"You need to know why you want to work with this client—do you want to make people's lives easier?" Desaulniers said. Or do you love creating art to add color to your world? Identifying these answers helps clarify your mission. Third, you want to determine how you are going to deliver that value to your customers and how to convey that value to your customers in a way that they are willing to pay for that value.

"Tip: To refine your business idea, define your "why", your target customers, and your business name.

During the ideation phase, the main details must be ironed out. If the idea isn't something you like or there isn't a market for your creation, it might be time to come up with another idea.

CHAPTER THREE

2. WRITE A BUSINESS PLAN

Once you have finalized your idea, you should ask yourself some important questions: What is the purpose of your business? Who do you sell to? What is your ultimate goal? How will you finance your startup costs? This question can be answered in a well-written business plan.

New businesses rush into things without thinking about this aspect of business. You need to find your target customer base. Who will buy your product or service? What if you can't prove there is demand for your idea?

Conduct market research.
Conducting thorough market research on your niche and potential customer demographics is an important part of creating a business plan. This includes conducting

surveys, focus groups, and SEO and social media research.

Market research helps you understand your target customers - their needs, wants and behaviors - your industry and your competitors. Many small business owners recommend collecting demographic data and conducting a competitive analysis to better understand the opportunities and limitations in your market.

The best small businesses have a product or service that sets them apart from the competition. This significantly affects your competitive landscape and allows you to provide unique value to potential customers.

See exit strategy.

It is also a good idea to consider an exit strategy when creating your business plan. Having some idea of how you're going to get out of the business forces you to look ahead.

"Often, new entrepreneurs are so excited about their business and believe there will be customers everywhere that they give themselves very little time to present an exit plan," said Josh Tolley, CEO of Shift Capital. and Kavanagh.

"When you get on the plane, what's the first thing you see? How to get out of it. When you go to the movies, what do they show before the feature starts playing? Out of the first Sunday of Kindergarten, all the children are lined up and learn fire drills to get out of the building. I have witnessed too many business leaders who do not have three or four predetermined exit routes. This leads to a decrease in the value of the company and even the breakdown of family relationships.

A business plan helps you know where your company is going, how it will overcome potential challenges, and what is needed to sustain it. When you're ready to put pencil to paper, these free templates can help.

CHAPTER FOUR

3. ASSESS YOUR FINANCES

Starting any business has a price, so you need to determine how you're going to cover those costs. Do you have the means to fund your startup, or will you need to borrow money? If you're planning to leave your current job to focus on your business, do you have money put away to support yourself until you make a profit? It's best to find out how much your startup costs will be.

Many startups fail because they run out of money before turning a profit. It's never a bad idea to overestimate the amount of startup capital you need, as it can be a while before the business begins to bring in sustainable revenue.

Perform a break-even analysis.
One way you can determine how much money you need is to perform a break-even

analysis. This is an essential element of financial planning that helps business owners determine when their company, product or service will be profitable.

The formula is simple:
Fixed Costs ÷ (Average Price − Variable Costs) = Break-Even Point
Every entrepreneur should use this formula as a tool because it informs you about the minimum performance your business must achieve to avoid losing money. Furthermore, it helps you understand exactly where your profits come from, so you can set production goals accordingly.

Here are the three most common reasons to conduct a break-even analysis:

Determine profitability. This is generally every business owner's highest interest.

Ask yourself: How much revenue do I need to generate to cover all my expenses? Which products or services turn a profit, and which ones are sold at a loss?

Price a product or service. When most people think about pricing, they consider how much their product costs to create and how competitors are pricing their products.
Ask yourself: What are the fixed rates, what are the variable costs, and what is the total cost? What is the cost of any physical goods? What is the cost of labor?

Analyze the data. What volumes of goods or services do you have to sell to be profitable? Ask yourself: How can I reduce my overall fixed costs? How can I reduce the variable costs per unit? How can I improve sales?

Watch your expenses.
Don't overspend when starting a business. Understand the types of purchases that make

sense for your business and avoid overspending on fancy new equipment that won't help you reach your business goals. Monitor your business expenses to ensure you are staying on track.

"A lot of startups tend to spend money on unnecessary things," said Jean Paldan, founder and CEO of Rare Form New Media. "We worked with a startup that had two employees but spent a huge amount on office space that would fit 20 people. They also leased a professional high-end printer that was more suited for a team of 100; it had key cards to track who was printing what and when. Spend as little as possible when you start, and only on the things that are essential for the business to grow and be a success. Luxuries can come when you're established."

Consider your funding options.
Startup capital for your business can come from various means. The best way to acquire

funding for your business depends on several factors, including creditworthiness, the amount needed and available options.

Business loans. If you need financial assistance, a commercial loan through a bank is a good starting point, although these are often difficult to secure. If you are unable to take out a bank loan, you can apply for a small business loan through the U.S. Small Business Administration (SBA) or an alternative lender. [Read related article: Best Alternative Small Business Loans]

Business Grants

Business grants are similar to loans; however, it is not refundable. Research grants are usually very competitive with terms and conditions that businesses must consider. When looking for small business grants, look for ones specific to your situation. Options include minority entrepreneurship grants, women's business grants, and government grants.

Investors. Startups that require significant upfront costs can bring investors. Investors can give start-up companies several million dollars or more, with the hope that the search engine will play an important role in making your business successful.

Pay a lot of money. Alternatively, you can start a crowdfunding campaign to collect a small amount of money from many supporters. Crowdfunding has helped many companies in recent years, and there are dozens of trusted crowdfunding platforms for various businesses.

You can learn more about each of these key sources and more in our guide to getting started with funding options.

Editor's Note: Looking for a small loan? Fill out the form below for our reseller partners to contact you about your needs.

Choose the right business bank.

When choosing a business bank, size matters. Marcus Anwar, co-founder of OhMy Canada, recommends small-market banks because they suit local market conditions and will work with you based on your overall business profile and personality.

"It's no different than the big banks that look at your credit score and are more selective about lending to small businesses," Anwar said. "Not only that, small banks want to build a personal relationship with you and help you if you have trouble and miss a payment. The good thing about small banks is that decisions are made at the branch level where decisions can be made faster than larger banks where decisions done at a higher level."

Anwar believes you should ask yourself these questions when choosing a bank for your business:

What is important to me?
Do I want to build a close relationship with a bank that wants to help me as much as possible?
Do I want to have another bank account like a big bank looking at me?
Ultimately, it comes down to the right bank for your business needs. Writing down your banking needs can help you focus on what you're looking for. Schedule meetings with different banks and ask questions about how they work with small businesses to find the best bank for your business. [Read Related Article: Business Bank Account Checklist: Required Documents]

Key Takeaway: Financially, you will want to do some due diligence, consider your costs and financing options, and choose the right bank for your business.

Intentionally left blank

CHAPTER FIVE

4. DETERMINE YOUR LEGAL BUSINESS STRUCTURE

Before registering your company, you need to determine what type of organization it is. If something goes wrong with your business, from your taxes to your personal liability, it has legal implications.

Sole Proprietorship. If you are the sole owner of the business and plan to be responsible for all debts and obligations, you can register as a sole proprietorship. Be warned that this route can directly affect your personal credit.
Work together. Alternatively, a business partnership, as the name suggests, means that two or more people are personally responsible as entrepreneurs. If you can find a business partner with complementary skills, you don't have to go it alone. This is usually a good idea to add to the mix to help your business thrive.

Corporation. If you want to separate your personal liability from the company's liability, you may want to consider forming some type of corporation (for example, an S corporation, a C corporation, or a B corporation). Although each type of corporation is subject to different regulations, this legal structure generally makes the business a separate entity from its owner, so the corporation can own property, bear liabilities, pay taxes, enter into contracts, sue, and other legal entities. . can. private. "Corporations, especially C corporations, are best suited for new businesses that plan to 'go public' or seek funding from venture capitalists," said Derrick Jordan, managing attorney at Jordan Council.

A limited liability company. One of the most common structures for small businesses is the limited liability company (LLC). This hybrid structure has the protection of corporate law while allowing for the tax benefits of the partnership.

Ultimately, it is up to you to decide which organization is best for your current needs and future business goals. It is important to learn about the different legal business structures available. If you're struggling to make a decision, it's not a bad idea to discuss the decision with a business or legal advisor.

Did you know: You need to choose a legal structure for your business, such as a sole proprietorship, partnership, corporation, or LLC.

Intentionally left blank

CHAPTER SIX

5. REGISTER WITH THE GOVERNMENT AND THE IRS

Before you can run a business legally, you need to obtain several business licenses. For example, you must register your business with federal, state, and local government agencies. There are some documents you need to prepare before you register.

Join the Operating Agreement

To become an officially recognized business entity, it must be registered with the government. Corporations need an 'articles of incorporation' document which includes your business name, business objectives, company structure, shareholding details and other information about your company. Likewise, some LLCs must create an operating agreement.

(DBA) to do business

If there are no articles of incorporation or operating agreement, you must register your business name, which can be your legal name, your default DBA name (if you have a sole proprietorship), or your maiden name. for your company You may also want to take steps to trademark your business name for additional legal protection.

Most states require you to obtain a DBA. If you are in a general partnership or sole proprietorship operating under a fictitious name, you can apply for a DBA certificate. It is best to contact or visit your local county clerk to ask about special requirements and fees. Generally, there is a registration fee.

Employer Identification Number (EIN)

After you register your business, you may need to obtain an employer identification number from the IRS. While this is not required for a sole proprietorship with no employees, you can hire one to keep personal and business taxes separate, or save yourself trouble if you decide to hire someone. The IRS has provided a checklist to determine if you need an EIN to run your business. If you need an EIN, you can register online for free.

Types of Income Tax

You will also need to file several forms to fulfill your federal and state income tax obligations. The form you need is determined by the structure of your business. You should check your state's website for information on state and local tax obligations.

"You might want to use PayPal accounts and social media platforms, but if you start with the right basics, you'll have less to worry about in the long run," says licensed attorney Nathalie Pierre-Louis. Owner of NPL Consultants.

Federal, state and local licenses and permits

Some businesses may also require federal, state, or local licenses and permits to operate. The best place to get a business license is at city hall. You can then use the SBA database to find licensing requirements by state and business type.

Businesses and independent contractors in some trades must obtain a professional license. An example of a professional license is a commercial driver's license (CDL). People with a CDL are allowed to operate several types of vehicles, such as buses, tanker trucks, and tractor trailers. CDLs are divided into three classes: Class A, Class B, and Class C.

You should also check with your city and state to find out if you need permission from the salesperson that authorizes you to collect taxes on your customers from your business. A dealer's permit goes by many names, including resale permit, resale license,

license permit, resale license, resale ID, state tax number, dealer number, dealer license, or license certificate.

It is important to note that these requirements and designations vary by country. With the seller's permission, you can register through the website of the state where you do business.
Not all businesses are required to collect sales tax (or obtain a vendor's permit), Jordan said.

"For example, many services (such as professional services, education and major home improvements), drugs or home consumption are not subject to sales tax in New York," Jordan said. "For example, if your business only sells drugs, you do not need a permit to sell in New York. But New York sales tax must be collected on the sale of new tangible personal goods, utilities, telephone services, hotel stays, and food and beverages (in restaurants). "

Important Documents: File important documents such as articles of incorporation or operating agreement, DBA, EIN, income tax forms, and other licenses and permits.

CHAPTER SEVEN

6. BUY AN INSURANCE POLICY

It may seem like you're finally "closer", but buying the right insurance for your business is an important step before you officially start working. Cases such as property damage, theft or customer lawsuits can be expensive to deal with, and you need to make sure you are properly protected.

While there are several types of business insurance to consider, there are some basic insurance plans that most small businesses can take advantage of. For example, if your business has employees, you should purchase compensation and unemployment insurance at a minimum.

Depending on your location and industry, you may need a different type, but most small businesses are advised to purchase general liability insurance (GL) or a business owner's policy. GL covers property damage, bodily injury and personal injury to yourself or a third party.

If your business provides services, you may want to consider professional indemnity insurance. It covers you if you do something wrong or neglect to do something while you are busy with your work.

CHAPTER EIGHT

7. BUILD YOUR TEAM

If you don't want to be the only employee, you need to recruit and hire a good team to get your company off the ground. Joe Zawadzki, CEO and founder of MediaMath, said entrepreneurs should pay attention to the equality of their products.

"Your product is built by people," Zawadzki said. "Identifying your editorial team, understanding what the gaps are, and determining how and when you will solve them should be your priority. Making sure the team will work together ... is equally important. Define roles and responsibilities, division of labor, how to respond , or working together when everyone is in the same room will save you a lot of headaches."

Intentionally left blank

CHAPTER NINE

8. CHOOSE YOUR DEALER

Running a business can be overwhelming, and you and your team can't do it alone. This is where third party vendors come in. From HR to business phone systems, companies in every industry are here to partner with you and make your business better.

When looking for a B2B partner, you need to choose carefully. These companies have access to important and potentially sensitive business information, so it's important to find someone you can trust. In our guide to choosing a business partner, our expert sources recommend asking potential vendors about their experience in your industry, their track record with existing clients, and how they've helped other clients grow.

Not every business needs the same vendor, but almost every business has the products and services they need. Consider the following functions that are necessary for all types of work.

Taking payments from customers: Offering multiple payment options will ensure that you are in the right format to sell to your target customers. You should compare options to find the right credit card provider to make sure you get the best rate for your business.

Financial Management: Many entrepreneurs can handle their own accounting functions when starting out, but as your business grows, you can save time by hiring an accountant or comparing accounting software.

CHAPTER TEN

9. BRAND AND PROMOTE YOURSELF

Before you start selling your products or services, you need to build your brand and find people who are ready to jump in when you open the door for business, whether live or mobile.

company website. Build your online reputation and build a company website. Most customers turn to the Internet to learn about business, and a website is digital proof that your small business exists. It's also a great way to stay connected with current and potential customers.

Social media. Use social media to spread the word about your new business, perhaps as a promotional tool to offer coupons and discounts to followers after you launch. The best social media platform will depend on your target audience.

CRM. The best CRM software solutions allow you to store customer data to improve the way you market to them. A well-thought-out email marketing campaign can do wonders to reach customers and connect with your audience. To be successful, you want to build your email marketing contact list strategically.

Logo. Create a logo that can help people easily identify your brand and use it consistently across all your platforms.

Also, update these digital assets with relevant and interesting content about your business and industry. According to Ruth Bowen, chief marketing officer of EastCamp Creative, many startups have misconceptions about websites.

"The point is to look at the website as an expense rather than an investment," Bowen said. "This is a big mistake in today's digital age. Small business owners who understand how important it is to have an online presence will have a leg up on a strong start."

Creating a marketing plan that goes beyond your business is essential to consistently getting the word out about your business and building a clientele. This process is as important as providing a quality product or service, especially in the beginning.

Ask customers to opt-in to your marketing communications.
As you build your brand, ask customers and potential customers for permission to contact you. The easiest way to do this is to use an optical image. According to Dan Edmonson, founder and CEO of Dronegenuity, this is a "consent form" submitted by web users.

"This type usually refers to email communication and is often used in e-commerce to ask customers for permission to send newsletters, marketing materials, product sales, etc.," says Edmonson. "People get a lot of junk e-mail and other messages these days, and you can build trust with your customers by being transparent about your services."

Opt-in forms are a great starting point for building trust and respect with potential customers. More importantly, these forms are required by law. The CAN-SPAM Act of 2003 sets forth the Federal Trade Commission's requirements for commercial e-mail. This law does not only apply to bulk emails; This law covers all commercial communications, which are defined as "commercial advertising or the primary purpose of promoting a commercial product or service." Each email that violates this law is subject to a $40,000 fine.

Tip: Create a strategic marketing campaign that integrates different marketing channels such as the company website, social media, email newsletters, and opt-in forms.

CHAPTER ELEVEN

10. GROW TOUR BUSINESS

Sales and initial sales are the beginning of your business as an entrepreneur. To generate income and stay afloat, you need to constantly grow your business. It takes time and effort, but what you put in, you get out. Working with well-known brands is a great way to promote your products. Reach out to other companies and ask for a few ads for free samples of their products or services. Partner with a charity and volunteer your time or products to get your name out there.

While these tips will help you launch and grow your business, no plan is perfect. You want to make sure you're ready to launch your business, but things will go wrong. To run a successful business, you need to adapt to changing circumstances.

"Get ready to fix it," says Stephanie Murray, founder of Fiddlestix Party + Supply. "There's a saying in the military, 'no plan survives first contact,' and it's probably the best plan in the world, but once you go, things change and you have to be ready, and as a broadcaster, to solve it. The problem is fast, your product or service for other people." Whether it's solving a problem or solving a problem in your organization, your problem is solved.

Questions about starting a business
How can I start my own business without money?
You can start a successful business without any start-up funds. Work on business ideas based on your skills to offer something new and innovative to the market. Keep working at your current position (or "day job") to reduce financial risk as you grow your new business.

Once you have developed your business idea and are ready to implement your business plan, you need to get creative with financing. You can raise money through investment by pitching your idea to a fund. You can also raise money through crowdfunding platforms like Kickstarter or put money from your weekly earnings to start a new business. Finally, you can look for loan options from banks and other financial institutions as a way to grow and manage your company.

Intentionally left blank

CHAPTER TWELVE

THE EASIEST BUSINESS TO START

What is the easiest business to start?

This is the easiest business to start, does not require financial investment and does not require extensive training to learn this business. One of the easiest ways to start a new business is as a spin-off company.

Dropshipping does not require inventory management, saving you the trouble of buying, storing and tracking stock. Instead, another company will fulfill your customer's order on your behalf. This company will manage the inventory, pack the items, and ship your work order. To get started, you can create an online store by choosing from a catalog of products available through partners.

When is the best time to start a business?

Everyone's ideal time to start a new job will be different. First, you should start working when you have enough time to concentrate. If you have a seasonal product or service, you'll want to start working one quarter of the year. For non-seasonal companies, spring and fall are popular times to start. Winter is the most popular start-up season, as many new owners prefer to get their business or company approved for the new fiscal year.

CHAPTER THIRTEEN

TIMING AND STARTING WORK

Check out some tips from StartupGrind founders who want to spread their knowledge to newbies like you. Here's what to say about timing and starting work:

1. If you have a jumping off point for your customers

If you're going to give the customer what they want, and let them say what they want. Julia Hartz of Eventbrite: "We strongly believe that many of our users are smarter than us. That does not mean that you can squeeze in additional products, business models, or commodities. However, remember that you do not have to have everything before you start. Your customers will think more Follow us on Twitter and stay updated on Eventbrite.

2. As soon as possible

According to Patrick Lee of Rotten Tomatoes, "start as soon as possible ... research is not very important." This doesn't mean you can just put together an average company and hope for the best. However, Lee is very balanced with the dreamer. Trust your instincts and you'll see when you dig your heels in for no reason. Check out the latest Rotten Tomatoes shows on Twitter.